Strong

Girl

Yoga for BUILDING STRENGTH

by Rebecca Rissman

CAPSTONE PRESS
a capstone imprint

Savvy Books are published by Capstone Press.
1710 Roe Crest Drive, North Mankato, Minnesota 56003
www.capstonepub.com

Library of Congress Cataloging-in-Publication Data

Cataloging-in-publication information is on file with the Library of Congress.

ISBN 978-1-4914-2122-2 (library binding)
ISBN 978-1-4914-2363-9 (eBook PDF)

Editorial Credits
Mandy Robbins, editor; Heidi Thompson, designer; Sarah Schuette, prop preparation; Marcy Morin, scheduler; Charmaine Whitman, production specialist

Photo Credits
Capstone Studio: TJ Thoraldson Digital Photography, all photos except; iStockphoto, Inc: Razvan, 5 (top); Shutterstock: AntonioDiaz, 58, Lucky Business, 56, Syda Productions, 61

Design Elements
Shutterstock: A-R-T, redstone, vectorkat

Printed in Canada.
092014   008478FRS15

TABLE OF *Contents*

WHAT IS YOGA?

What kind of girl do you want to be—fit, strong, smart, or chill? Look no further. You don't need to go to gyms or fitness centers filled with high-tech exercise machines. You don't need to wear a tiny computer on your shoe to record running distance and speed. You can become everything you want to be by doing one very low-tech activity—yoga.

Yoga is an ancient practice that comes from India. It involves working on the physical body, the mind, and the spirit through careful practice and determination. The word "yoga" comes from the Sanskrit word *Yuj*, which means "to unite, or join." Many people who practice yoga believe it helps them to unite and balance their body, mind, and spirit.

Yoga has many benefits. Some people practice yoga because it helps them feel less stressed or anxious. Others use yoga to improve their flexibility and strength. Yoga can even boost your brainpower. Whatever your goals, yoga can help you achieve them. Get ready to become the girl you've always wanted to be.

Today's fitness experts are starting to focus on one low-tech practice: yoga.

Many people who practice yoga believe it helps them to unite and balance their body, mind, and spirit.

Asana

Pronounced: AH-sah-nah

From the root word *as*, meaning "to sit," or "to be"

Asana is a word you'll hear over and over during your yoga practice. This Sanskrit term is used to describe a yoga pose. Most yoga poses are named after animals, objects, or familiar motions. For example, *ustrasana* means "Camel Pose." *Ustra* is the Sanskrit word for "camel."

FINDING
Strength
IN YOGA

Strength training is a type of exercise that builds up muscle and bone. Even though yoga doesn't involve lifting weights or using fitness machines, it's a great strength training workout. Yoga uses the best strength training tool you have—your own body weight.

Yoga involves isometric strength training. Isometric exercises challenge your muscles to work by holding a weight-bearing position without moving. This means your muscles must stay still in a tensed position. Most yoga classes involve holding different poses for several breaths at a time. At first, the poses might seem simple or even easy. But after a few breaths, the isometric challenge of holding the poses will have you sweating.

Yoga doesn't just strengthen your muscles. It can also strengthen your bones. Over time, our bones can become weaker and more fragile. Activities such as yoga, that encourage safe weight-bearing postures, can help bones stay strong over time.

Almost all types of yoga that involve asanas, or physical poses, can help you increase your strength. One type of yoga is called Ashtanga. It is a vigorous and high-energy practice that involves moving through a series of very challenging poses. Many practitioners of Ashtanga Yoga practice up to six times a week.

Stay Safe.

Yoga can be a safe, gentle way to build muscle and bone strength if you follow one rule: Never stay in a pose that feels painful. When performed correctly, a yoga pose might make you feel a deep stretch or muscular challenge. But it should never, ever cause pain.

Guru

Pronounced GOO-roo

From the root word *gri*, meaning "to praise"

Guru is a Sanskrit word that means "teacher," or "leader." Many types of yoga were developed by different gurus over time. For example, Ashtanga Yoga was developed by a guru named Pattabhi Jois. People all over the world follow his teachings.

TRIANGLE POSE

Sanskrit Name: *Utthita Trikonasana*

Pronunciation: ooh-TEE-tah tree-kon-AHS-ah-nah

Practicing yoga regularly is one of the best ways to maintain a healthy, strong back. Triangle Pose works the muscles in the back while it stretches the neck, legs, shoulders, and feet.

step 1 Stand at the front of your yoga mat. Turn to face the left. Take a big step back with your right foot to bring your feet at least 3 feet (1 meter) apart.

step 2 With straight legs, turn your right toes to point toward the front of your mat. Angle your left foot so that the toes point toward the left front corner of your mat. Point both sides of your hips toward the left side of your mat.

step 3 Extend your arms out to the sides, with palms facing down.

step 4 Pull your shoulder blades closer together. Drop your shoulders away from your ears.

Keep both legs as straight as possible without locking your knees.

step 5 Reach your left fingertips down to rest on your left shin, the floor outside your left foot, or a yoga block.

step 6 Repeat on the other side.

step 7 Hold for several breaths.

Reach your right arm straight up with your palm facing the right side of your mat.

Look straight ahead or challenge yourself by looking up toward your fingers.

Stack your right shoulder over your left shoulder.

9

REVOLVED TRIANGLE

Revolved Triangle takes the stretching and strengthening benefits of Triangle Pose and adds a challenging twist. It can be tough to balance in this pose, so remember to focus your gaze on something close by.

Sanksrit Name: *Parvrtta Trikonasana*

Pronunciation:

par-VREE-tah tree-kon-AHS-ah-nah

Keep both legs as straight as possible without locking your knees.

step 1   Stand at the front of your yoga mat. Turn to face the right. Take a step back with your right foot to bring your feet about 2.5 feet (0.75 m) apart.

step 2   Slightly bend your left knee and turn your left toes to point toward the front of your mat. Keeping your right leg straight, angle your right foot so that the toes point toward the right front corner of your mat. Press your left heel firmly down into the mat.

step 3   Bring your hands to your hips and square your hips to the front of your yoga mat. To do this, pull your right hip forward and push your left hip back. Point your belly button forward.

step 4   Lift the crown of your head straight up to lengthen your back.

step 5   Bend at the hips to bring your right hand down to the mat just outside your left foot. Keep your left hand on your left hip. If this twist feels too difficult, bring your right hand to the inside of your left foot instead.

step 6   Slowly begin to straighten your left knee. If this feels too challenging, rest your right fingertips on a block instead of the floor.

step 7   Raise your left arm straight up. Straighten the elbow and face the palm toward the left side of your mat.

step 8   Lift your right ear away from your right shoulder so that your head and neck are in line with your spine. Take three breaths.

step 9   Repeat on the other side.

WARRIOR 3 POSE

Sanskrit Name: *Virabhadrasana 3*

Pronunciation: veer-ah-bah-DRAHS-ah-nah

Warrior 3 Pose can improve your back strength, shoulder flexibility, balance, and focus.

step 1 If you're using a mat, start this pose standing at the back of it. Step your right foot at least 3 feet (1 m) forward. Keep your right toes pointing straight ahead.

step 2 Bend the right knee deeply until it is over the ankle. Lift your arms straight up toward the sky with your palms facing one another.

step 3 Reach your arms forward with straight elbows as you stand on your right foot and extend your left.

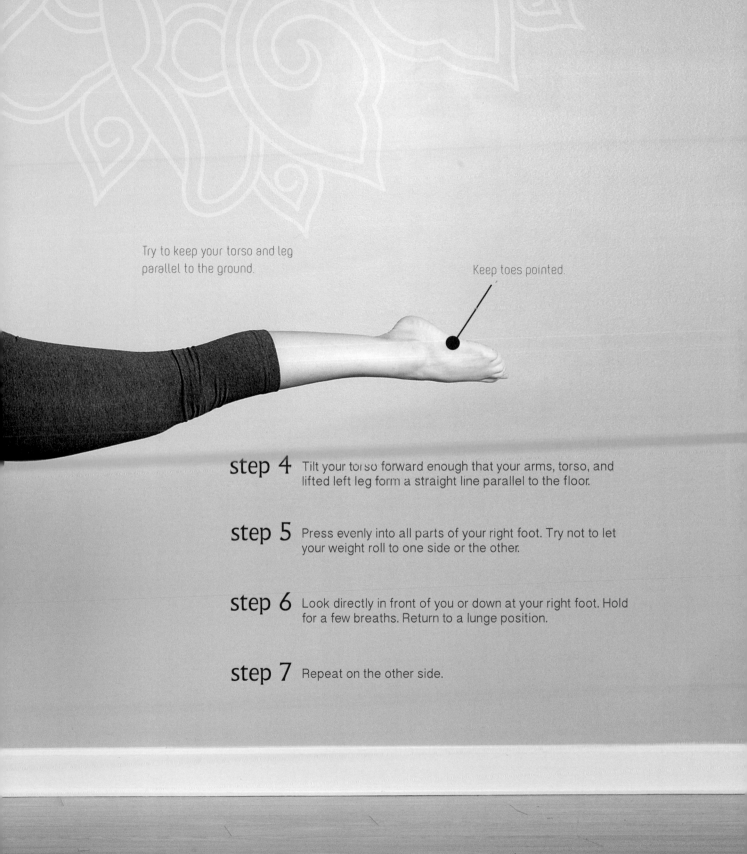

Try to keep your torso and leg parallel to the ground.

Keep toes pointed.

step 4 Tilt your torso forward enough that your arms, torso, and lifted left leg form a straight line parallel to the floor.

step 5 Press evenly into all parts of your right foot. Try not to let your weight roll to one side or the other.

step 6 Look directly in front of you or down at your right foot. Hold for a few breaths. Return to a lunge position.

step 7 Repeat on the other side.

STANDING SPLITS

Sanskrit Name: *Urdhva Prasarita Eka Padasana*

Pronunciation: OOR-dvah prah-sah-REE-ta EH-kah pah-DAS-ah-nah

If you're ready for a real challenge, try mastering the Standing Splits. It's a deep stretch for the standing leg and a great workout for the muscles in your back. Pay attention to which side is easier for you. Most people are more flexible on one side than the other.

step 1 Stand with your feet 4 to 5 inches (10 to 13 cm) apart. Have your toes slightly closer together than your heels.

step 2 Bend at the hips to fold forward. Let both hands dangle toward the floor. If you are able to, rest your fingertips on the mat in front of your feet. If you can't reach the floor, rest your hands on blocks instead.

step 3 Lean your weight into your left foot. Lift your right leg behind you.

→ An advanced version of this pose adds the challenge of balance. Once you've mastered the Standing Splits with your hands on the floor or on blocks, try it with one or both hands resting on the ankle of the standing leg.

Flex your foot.

step 4 Straighten your right knee as much as possible and flex your foot to point your toes toward the floor. Lift your right heel away from the floor.

step 5 Draw your upper body closer to your left leg as you fold forward even more. Hold for a few breaths.

step 6 Repeat on the other side.

CHAIR POSE

Sanskrit Name: *utkatasana*

Pronounced: oot-kah-TAS-ah-nah

Do you want to strengthen the muscles in your feet, calves, thighs, buns, and back all at once? Try Chair Pose. Who knew taking a seat could be so challenging?

step 1 Place feet 4 to 5 inches (10 to 13 cm) apart, with your toes slightly closer together than your heels.

step 2 Bend the knees deeply, as though you are going to sit down into a chair.

step 3 With straight elbows, raise your arms up. Try to align your upper arms with your ears.

step 4 Rock your weight back into your heels so that your hips are hovering over your heels.

step 5 Draw your upper body closer to your legs as you fold forward even more. Hold for a few breaths.

step 6 Release pose and repeat several times.

Keep your chin
parallel to the floor.

17

HIGH LUNGE

Few people can agree on the proper Sanskrit name for this pose.
But no one denies that it's a great pose for strengthening your legs.

step 1 From a standing position, take a big step forward with your left leg. Point your left toes straight ahead.

step 2 Bend the left knee deeply while you keep your right leg as straight as you can. Lift your right heel away from the floor so that you are resting on the ball of your right foot.

step 3 Raise both arms up with your palms facing in.

step 4 Try not to allow your shoulders to rise up near your ears. Focus on dropping them down toward the floor. Roll your shoulder blades up and then down toward your bottom.

step 5 Square your hips. To do this, point your hips and belly button toward the front of the room or yoga mat. Hold for several breaths.

step 6 Repeat on the other side.

Think carefully about your feet in this pose. Press your left big toe down especially hard. Doing this will help you prevent any injuries to your knees while holding this pose.

Face your palms in.

Knee Safety

Keep your knees healthy and safe by always following this rule: Whenever you are bending your knee in a lunging pose, make sure the knee stays above the ankle. If you allow your knee to balance farther forward, above your toes, you might put too much stress on the joint.

Square your hips.

Keep your back leg as straight as you can.

Lift your heel away from the floor.

HORSE POSE

Sanskrit Name: *Utkata Konasana*

Pronounced: OOT-kah-tah kone-AHS-ah-nah

Also known as Goddess Pose, this asana is a good way to gain flexibility in the hips while you strengthen your thighs.

step 1 Take a wide stance, with your heels about 3 feet (1 m) apart. Turn both feet out, so that your toes point out and your heels point in.

step 2 Bend your knees deeply. Try to bring your knees just above your heels.

step 3 Keep your upper body upright. Point your tailbone down and try to balance your shoulders above your hips.

step 4 Bring your palms together in front of your heart. Hold for several breaths.

step 5 Slowly straighten your legs to come out of the pose safely.

 Try not to lean forward in this pose. Imagine you are pressing your back up against a wall.

BRIDGE POSE

Sanskrit Name: *Setu Bandha Sarvangasana*

Pronounced: SET-too BAN-da sar-vahn-GAS-ah-nah

Try to imagine your body forming the shape of a bridge over a small stream. That's the idea behind the aptly named Bridge Pose.

Press your hands into the mat.

step 1   Lay down on your back.

step 2   Bend your knees and bring your heels close to your bottom. Your feet should be 2 to 3 inches (5 to 8 cm) apart and parallel to one another. Rest your arms down along your sides.

step 3   Press your feet down as you lift your hips up. Keeping your arms at your sides, press them down into your yoga mat. Press the back of your head down into your yoga mat. Try not to let your knees fall out, away from each other. They should stay about 3 inches (8 cm) apart during this pose.

step 4   After a few breaths, slowly lie down onto your back again.

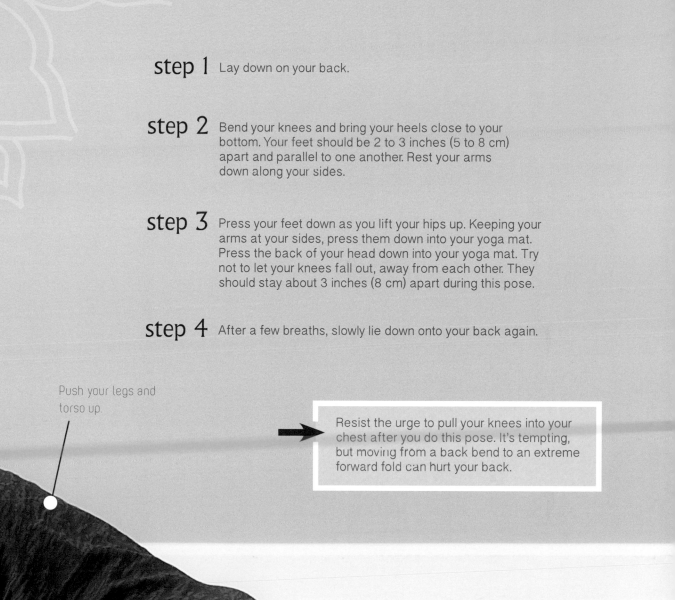

Push your legs and torso up.

Resist the urge to pull your knees into your chest after you do this pose. It's tempting, but moving from a back bend to an extreme forward fold can hurt your back.

DOLPHIN POSE

Dolphin Pose is a challenging but safe way to work your arms, shoulders, core, and back. It doesn't have a commonly used Sanskrit name, but it's still part of a balanced yoga practice.

step 1 Start on your hands and knees. From there, drop your forearms to the mat. Make sure your forearms are parallel to one another, and your palms are facing down on the mat.

step 2 With your feet 3 to 4 inches (8 to 10 cm) apart, tuck your toes under. Press into the balls of your feet to lift your knees off of the mat and point your bottom up. If this feels challenging for you, stay in this posture for several breaths and then take a break.

step 3 If you want to try a deeper form of this pose, work on straightening your legs as much as you can by pressing your bottom up toward the sky.

Press your heels toward the ground.

Enter this pose slowly and listen to your body. If you feel any pain, stop immediately.

step 4 Press your chest toward the space between your knees.

step 5 Relax your neck by allowing your head to hang loosely. Your head should not touch the yoga mat.

step 6 Hold for several breaths.

step 7 Bring your knees down to the mat and press back up to your hands to safely come out of this pose.

If full Dolphin Pose is too challenging for you, stop at Step 2. In this slightly easier version, the knees stay bent.

FOREARM PLANK

If you want a quick way to strengthen your arms, shoulders, core, and back, the Forearm Plank is the pose for you. This pose can quickly tire you, so try to hold it for a few breaths. Then, take a break before trying it again.

step 1 Start out on your hands and knees. From there, bring your forearms to the mat. Make sure they are parallel to one another, and your palms are facing down.

step 2 Stretch both legs out behind you, and tuck your toes. Your heels should rise straight up away from the floor, and the balls of both feet will hold your weight.

step **3** Straighten your legs, and press your tailbone toward your heels. This will help your back stay very straight.

step **4** Pull your shoulders away from your ears and look down between your hands.

step **5** Hold for several breaths, then return to your hands and knees to rest.

Try to keep your back as straight as possible.

If this pose feels too difficult or puts pressure on your lower back, try bringing your knees down to the mat. Keep your bottom low to form a straight line from your knees to your head.

UPWARD FACING PLANK

Sanskrit Name: *Purvottanasana*

Pronounced: purr-voh-ton-AH-sah-nah

Purvottanasana means "intense stretch of the East." While the stretch may be tough, this pose is also an excellent and safe way to strengthen your arms. Make sure to work on finding the correct alignment, or body positioning, in this pose. Safe alignment is the best way to avoid injuries in yoga.

step 1 From a seated position, place your hands a few inches behind your hips with your fingers facing forward. Straighten your arms.

step 2 With bent knees, place your feet on the mat about 1.5 feet (0.5 m) in front of your bottom.

step 3 Lift your bottom off of the mat so that it is at the same height as your knees and shoulders.

Keep your feet as flat as possible.

step 4 One leg at a time, slide your heels forward to straighten each leg. Point your toes so that your feet are as flat on the mat as possible.

step 5 If it feels comfortable, allow your head to drop by relaxing your neck. Hold for a few breaths.

step 6 Carefully lower your bottom down to the mat and rest.

Drop your head back.

Face your fingers forward.

L-POSE

So you think you have this "yoga" thing down? Why not challenge yourself with L-Pose. You might want a friend to help you out when you first try this pose.

Some very advanced yoga students do handstands as part of their practice. L-Pose is also referred to as "Half-Handstand" because it helps prepare people to work toward doing handstands by building shoulder and back strength.

step 1 Sit against a wall with your bottom pressed against the floorboards and your legs outstretched and straight. Use a towel, water bottle, or other handy item to mark where your heels are on the floor. This way, you know exactly how far one leg-length away from the wall is.

step 2 Come onto your hands and knees with the base of your palms lined up with the marker you used. Place your hands shoulder-distance apart on the floor and point your index fingers straight ahead. Straighten your arms.

step 3 Tuck your toes and place the balls of your feet against the floorboards behind you.

continue on page 32 ➡

step 4 Slowly start to walk your feet up the wall. Stop when they reach the height of your hips.

step 5 Press your chest toward the wall. Keep your hands flat on the floor and your elbows straight.

Keep your legs parallel to the ground.

step 6 Press your legs as straight as you can. Tighten your stomach muscles, and relax your neck so that your head can hang loosely.

step 7 Hold for a few breaths. Then walk your feet down the wall to rest.

BOW POSE

Sanskrit Name: *Dhanurasana*

Pronounced: don-yur-AH-san-ah

In Bow Pose your body takes the shape of an archer's bow. Not only does this pose give you an intense stretch, but it also strengthens your shoulders at the same time.

step 1   Lie on your belly with your arms down at your sides and your forehead resting on the mat.

step 2   Bend your knees to bring your feet close to your bottom. Reach back and grasp the outer edges of your ankles. Try not to let your knees flop out to the sides when you do this.

Flex your feet.

step 2

step 3 Roll your shoulders up and back. Gently lift your head away from your mat and start to kick your heels away from your bottom. This will pull your shoulders farther away from the mat. It will also begin to lift your thighs off the floor.

step 4 Breathe gently and focus on an object in front of you to stay centered.

step 5 Slowly release your ankles and straighten your legs out on the mat. Rest your forehead on the mat. Allow your hands to fall comfortably at your sides.

Having trouble grabbing your ankles? Don't worry. Wrap a towel or yoga strap around your ankles and hold onto that instead.

EAGLE POSE

Sanskrit Name: *Garudasana*

Pronounced: gah-roo-dah-AH-san-ah

Eagle Pose combines several challenging elements. Not only does it ask your muscles to hold a tricky position for several breaths, but it also requires you to balance at the same time.

step 1 Stand with your feet 2 to 3 inches (5 to 8 cm) apart. Have your toes slightly closer together than your heels. Let your arms hang at your sides.

step 2 Bend both knees deeply. Lift your left foot off the floor and cross your left knee over your right. If you can, hook your left toes behind your right calf.

step 3 Keeping your legs crossed, bring your arms out to your sides with your palms facing forward.

step 4 Reach your arms forward and cross your left elbow under your right. Bend both elbows to reach your hands up toward the ceiling. If you are able, bring your palms together.

step 5 Keep your knees bent and rock your weight into your right heel. Lift your elbows so that they are at the same height as your shoulders. Look straight ahead. Hold for a few breaths.

step 6 Slowly uncross your legs and arms, and stand on both feet. Repeat this pose on the other side.

Your sight plays a big role in finding balance. Try this experiment: Do Eagle Pose while looking at a steady object a few feet in front of you. Try Eagle Pose again with your eyes closed. Which version was more challenging for you?

EXTENDED SIDE ANGLE POSE

Sanskrit Name: *Utthita Parsvakonasana*

Pronounced: OOH-teet-ah pars-voh-koe-NAH-san-ah

Extended Side Angle Pose works your shoulders as well as your legs, core, and back. This pose will strengthen your whole body.

step 1 From a standing position, take a big step forward with your left leg. Point your left toes straight ahead.

step 2 Bend the left knee deeply while you keep your right leg as straight as you can. Turn your right heel down so that your whole foot is touching the mat.

For the most advanced version of this pose, place your left hand outside your left foot for a deep side stretch.

Try to form a straight line from your toes to your fingertips.

step 3 Bring your left elbow to your left thigh. If this feels challenging, stay here. If you want more of a stretch, bring your left fingertips to the mat outside of your left foot.

step 4 Reach your right arm up. Open your chest to the right side of your mat. Then slowly reach your right arm forward until it is in the same line as your right leg. Turn your palm down toward the floor. Hold for a few breaths.

step 5 Repeat on the other side.

BOAT POSE

Sanskrit Name: *Navasana*

Pronounced: nah-VAS-ah-nah

The core muscles are those that surround your hips, belly, and low back. Almost all yoga poses work the muscles in your core. However, some poses challenge these muscles more than others. Boat Pose is a wonderful core exercise.

step 1 Sit on your mat with your legs outstretched in front of you. Reach your arms forward, with your palms facing in.

step 2 Slowly lean back until your legs feel very heavy. Then bend your knees up toward the sky until you are resting on your heels and bottom. Keep reaching your arms forward.

Keep your chin up.

Your arms should be parallel with your legs.

Keep your back as straight as possible.

Yogi and Yogini

Pronounced: YO-gee and yoh-GEE-nee

From the root *Yuj*, meaning, "one who is joined or connected"

You might hear yoga teachers referring to *yogis* and *yoginis*. Who are they talking about? *Yogi* is the term used to describe male yoga students. *Yogini* is the term for female yoga students.

step 3 With your knees bent, lift your heels off the ground. If this feels difficult, remain in this position. If you want more of a challenge, raise your heels until your shins are parallel to the floor.

step 4 Hold for a few breaths.

step 5 Slowly lower your heels to the mat and return to a seated position to rest.

For the most advanced version of this pose, straighten your legs. Your body will form the shape of a V.

Straighten your legs as much as you can.

BIRD DOG POSE

When you are doing Bird Dog Pose, you might not feel your core muscles working, but they are. This seemingly simple pose works the muscles in your abdomen, lower back, upper back, and legs.

step 1 Start on your hands and knees. Have your knees the same width as your hips, and have your hands directly beneath your shoulders.

step 2 Firm the muscles of your belly by pulling your belly button in toward your spine.

step 3 Extend your left arm forward with your palm facing in. Straighten your elbow.

Flex your top foot.

Tuck your bottom toes under.

step 4 Tuck your left toes under. Then extend your right leg straight behind you. Your right toes should point straight down. Straighten your knee as much as you can.

step 5 Do not allow your belly to fall down toward the mat. If you feel this happening, keep pulling your belly button in toward your spine.

step 6 Look straight down at your yoga mat. Hold for a few breaths.

step 7 Repeat on the other side.

Face your palm in.

Look straight down.

SIDE PLANK

Sanskrit Name: *Vasisthasana*

Pronounced: vash-eesh-TAS-ah-nah

Side Plank is a fun variation on Plank Pose. The full version of this pose challenges you to use only one hand and the edge of one foot to balance. If this feels too difficult, don't be afraid to modify the pose.

step 1   Start out in full Plank Pose with knees lifted away from the floor.

Form one straight line with your arms and another from your head to your toes.

step 2   Roll your weight onto the outer edge of your right foot, and stack your left foot on top of your right. At the same time, lift your left arm straight up with the palm facing forward.

step 3 Press your hips upward so that your body forms a straight line from the crown of your head down through your heels. Hold for a few breaths.

step 4 Return to Plank Pose by dropping the lifted hand and foot to the mat.

step 5 Bend your knees to rest on your hands and knees.

step 6 Repeat on the other side.

For a slightly easier version of the pose, try bending your right knee and stepping your right foot directly in front of the left knee.

HALF MOON POSE

Sanskrit Name: *Ardha Chandrasana*

Pronounced: ARE-duh chon-DRAS-ah-nah

Half Moon Pose is an excellent way to work your legs, feet, back, and the sides of your abdomen. It's also a challenging pose for balance.

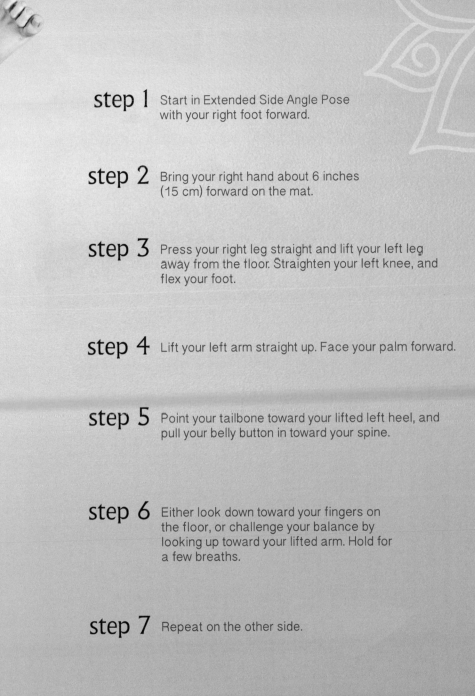

step 1 Start in Extended Side Angle Pose with your right foot forward.

step 2 Bring your right hand about 6 inches (15 cm) forward on the mat.

step 3 Press your right leg straight and lift your left leg away from the floor. Straighten your left knee, and flex your foot.

step 4 Lift your left arm straight up. Face your palm forward.

step 5 Point your tailbone toward your lifted left heel, and pull your belly button in toward your spine.

step 6 Either look down toward your fingers on the floor, or challenge your balance by looking up toward your lifted arm. Hold for a few breaths.

step 7 Repeat on the other side.

TREE POSE

Sanskrit Name: *Vrksasana*

Pronounced: vrik-SHASH-ah-nah

You might not think of them often, but the muscles in your feet are very important for the health of your knees, back, and even core. Tree Pose is an excellent muscular workout for your feet.

step 1 Stand with your feet 4 to 5 inches (10 to 13 cm) apart. Have your toes slightly closer together than your heels. Bring your hands to your hips.

step 2 Lean your weight into your right foot. Bring the sole of your left foot into the inside of the right ankle, calf, or thigh. Do not allow the sole of the left foot to rest against the right knee. Doing so could put pressure on your knee, causing injury. The higher up you rest your foot, the more challenging the pose.

step 3 Reach both arms above your head. Straighten your elbows and face your palms toward one another.

step 4 Either gaze forward, or as a challenge, try to look up. Hold for a few breaths.

step 5 Return to a standing position.

step 6 Repeat on the other side.

GARLAND POSE

Sanskrit Name: *Malasana*

Pronounced: mal-AHS-an-ah

Garland Pose is a simple squat stretch. It stretches your hips and thighs while strengthening your back and feet.

step 1   Stand with your feet about 4 to 5 inches (10 to 13 cm) apart. Turn your toes out to the side.

step 2   Bend your knees to come into a deep squatting position. Allow your knees to open up to the sides.

step 3   Try to keep your heels on the ground. If this feels like too deep of a stretch, take your feet farther apart and try again.

step 4   Bring your palms together in front of your heart. Press your elbows against the inside edges of both knees.

step 5   Straighten your back as much as you can. Lift your chin slightly away from your chest. Hold for a few breaths.

A simple way to modify this pose is to roll up a towel or yoga blanket and place it under your heels. This will make the stretch less intense in your feet.

EXTENDED HAND-TO-TOE POSE

Sanskrit Name: *Utthita Hasta Padangustasana*

Pronounced: ooh-TEE-tah HAH-sta pah-dahn-goo-STAS-ah-nah

Many yoga poses use binds. Binds are arm positions in which the hands clasp one another, or grasp a body part. Binds work the muscles in the hands. Extended Hand-to-Toe Pose is a nice way to strengthen your hands and work on balance at the same time.

step 1 Stand with your feet 4 to 5 inches (10 to 13 cm) apart. Have your toes slightly closer together than your heels. Bring your right hand to your right hip.

step 2 Lean your weight into your right leg. Lift your left foot off the ground and bring your left knee up in front of your hip.

step 3 Grasp your left big toe with the index and middle fingers of your left hand. Slowly extend your left leg out in front of you as much as you can. Don't worry if your leg doesn't become completely straight.

step 4 Keeping your gaze locked on something in front of you, slowly bring your left leg out to the left. Keep your hips facing forward.

If this stretch feels too intense, modify this pose. Instead of grasping the left toes, hold on to the outer edge of your left knee. Keep your knee bent and back straight as you open your left leg out to the side.

Keep your leg as
straight as possible.

step 5 Hold for a few breaths.

step 6 Repeat on the other side.

DANCER POSE

Sanskrit Name: *Natarajasana*

Pronounced: nah-tar-ah-JAS-ah-nah

Dancer Pose challenges your balance, flexibility, and the muscles in your hands—all at the same time. Try this pose holding a wall or chair if you find it difficult to balance.

step 1 Stand with your feet 4 to 5 inches (10 to 13 cm) apart. Have your toes slightly closer together than your heels. Reach your left arm straight up into the sky.

step 2 Lean your weight into your right leg. Kick your left foot toward your bottom, and grasp the outer edge of your left foot with your left hand.

step 3 Point your left knee straight down toward the floor. Try to keep your left knee from opening out to the left.

step 4 Slowly start to press your left foot into your left hand. Your heel will come away from your bottom as you start to stretch.

step 5 Carefully begin to lean your upper body forward and reach your right arm straight out in front of you, palm facing down. Hold for a few breaths.

step 6 Slowly and carefully lift your upper body to an upright position and release your lifted left foot to the floor.

step 7 Repeat on the other side.

Clasp the outside of your foot.

If it's difficult to grab your left foot with your left hand, hold a towel or yoga strap wrapped around your ankle instead.

WHERE CAN YOU DO *Yoga?*

If you are interested in building strength with yoga, a yoga studio is a great place to start. Yoga studios often feature many different types of classes and teachers. Some gyms also have yoga classes in their fitness or aerobic studios. Look for classes with names like Power Yoga, Yoga Flow, Vinyasa Yoga, and Yoga for Athletes. These active classes will highlight strength building poses.

If you don't live near a gym or yoga studio, don't worry. You can do yoga anywhere, at any time. Yoga mats, yoga clothes, and yoga props are nice, but they aren't necessary. All you really need to practice yoga is a quiet place with a flat, level area. Experiment with different poses. If something feels challenging or makes your muscles sore, keep working on it. Soon, your muscles will grow stronger, and the poses you find difficult will become easier.

If you're a beginner, start slowly. Gather a group of friends and try beginning poses together. Ask a trusted adult to help you find a safe website that shows yoga teachers doing different poses. There are even some websites that feature videos of entire yoga classes for you to try. When you become more experienced, you can have fun experimenting with different poses.

Yoga is a great activity to try outdoors. Why not grab your girlfriends and enjoy nature while working to strengthen your muscles and bones? You can practice in your own yard or a nearby park.

If you choose to do yoga alone at your home, make sure to be safe. Never try any poses beyond your skill level. Advanced poses may look easy in photos, but they could cause injury if done incorrectly. And always remember to stop what you're doing if you feel pain in any pose.

Don't Fall In!

In some places, you can even do yoga on the water. Stand Up Paddleboard yoga classes are becoming very popular. In these classes, yogis and yoginis work on holding poses while balancing on a wide type of surfboard. The motion of the water makes holding stationary poses very challenging. Just imagine doing a headstand while floating.

Try keeping a yoga journal. Record the poses you are working on and how they make you feel physically and mentally. Record where and how often you are practicing yoga. Take notes on which poses challenge your muscles, your flexibility, and your focus. If you find yourself feeling frustrated or distracted in your yoga practice, take a moment to record these feelings in your journal as well.

Before long, you might notice that the poses you struggled with at the beginning of your yoga journey have become easy. Reserve a special section of your yoga journal where you can write down any poses you hope to learn one day.

Find a way of practicing yoga that fits you and your personality. Whether it's a class in a gym, yoga in the park, or even practicing alone in your bedroom, it's important to find a style of yoga that you enjoy. After all, the more fun you have, the more likely you will be to stick with yoga and become a stronger you.

Build Mental Muscle

Yoga doesn't just challenge your muscles. It also challenges your mind. Because yoga doesn't usually involve loud music or fast movements, it can be difficult to concentrate on each pose. Try your best to keep your mind focused on your physical movements. When you notice that your mind is wandering, don't get discouraged. Just stop and close your eyes. Think about your breath and your physical alignment. Then open your eyes and try focusing again.

Glossary

alignment (uh-LYNE-muhnt)—the correct positioning of the body in order to reduce the chance of injury

core (KOHR)—the muscles of your stomach, chest, back, and pelvis

inversion (in-VUR-zhun)—type of pose in which the head is brought below the heart; standing forward folds, headstands, and handstands are all considered inversions.

isometric (eye-soh-MET-rick)—muscle activity in which a tensed position is held steady

modification (mah-duh-fih-KAY-shuhn)—a change made to a yoga pose in order to better suit a particular person's body

pelvis (PEL-vis)—large bones found at the base of the abdomen

prop (PROP)—a tool used to make different yoga poses easier

Sanskrit (SAN-skrit)—an ancient language from India written from left to right in a script called Devangari

torso (TOR-so)—the part of the body between the neck and waist, not including the arms

READ MORE

Burns, Brian, Howard Kent, and Claire Hayler. *Yoga for Beginners.* From Couch to Conditioned: A Beginner's Guide to Getting Fit. New York: Rosen Pub., 2011.

Purperhart, Helen. *Yoga Exercises for Teens: Developing a Calmer Mind and a Stronger Body.* Alameda, Calif.: Hunter House Publishers, 2009.

Spilling, Michael. *Yoga Step-By-Step.* Skills in Motion. New York: Rosen Central, 2011.

Wood, Alix. *You Can Do Yoga.* Let's Get Moving! Gareth Stevens Publishing: New York, 2014.

INTERNET SITES

FactHound offers a safe, fun way to find Internet sites related to this book. All of the sites on FactHound have been researched by our staff.

Here's all you do:

Visit *www.facthound.com*

Type in this code: 9781491421222

ABOUT THE AUTHOR

Rebecca Rissman is a certified yoga instructor, nonfiction author, and editor. She has written books about history, culture, science, and art. Her book *Shapes in Sports* earned a starred review from *Booklist* magazine, and her series *Animal Spikes and Spines* received *Learning Magazine*'s 2013 Teachers Choice for Children's Books. She lives in Portland, Oregon, with her husband and daughter, and enjoys hiking, yoga, and cooking.

Index